W9-BLF-694

Date Due

THE ENCYCLOPEDIA OF PSYCHOACTIVE DRUGS

IN 25 VOLUMES
Each title on a specific drug or drug-related problem

TEENAGE DEPRESSION AND SUICIDE

THE ENCYCLOPEDIA OF PSYCHOACTIVE DRUGS

TEENAGE DEPRESSION AND SUICIDE

JOHN CHILES, M.D.

University of Washington Medical School

1986
CHELSEA HOUSE PUBLISHERS
NEW YORK
NEW HAVEN   PHILADELPHIA

SENIOR EDITOR: William P. Hansen
PROJECT EDITOR: Jane Larkin Crain
ASSISTANT EDITOR: Paula Edelson
EDITORIAL COORDINATOR: Karyn Gullen Browne
EDITORIAL STAFF: Jeff Freiert
               Perry Scott King
               Kathleen McDermott
               Alma Rodriguez-Sokol
CAPTIONS: Norman Plotkin
ART DIRECTOR: Susan Lusk
ART COORDINATOR: Carol McDougall
LAYOUT: Victoria Tomaselli
ART ASSISTANT: Noreen M. Lamb
PICTURE RESEARCH: Elizabeth Terhune
               Andrea Bonasera

COVER: *Head of a Man* by Pablo Picasso, SES/Art Resource

First printing

Library of Congress Cataloging in Publication Data
Chiles, John.
    Teenage depression and suicide.

    (The Encyclopedia of psychoactive drugs)
    Bibliography: p.
    Includes index.
    Summary: Examines the causes of teen-age depression
and suicide and the role drugs play in the emotional
upheavals of young people.
    1. Youth—Suicidal behavior—Juvenile literature.
2. Youth—Drug use—Juvenile literature. 3. Adolescent
psychology—Juvenile literature. 4. Depression,
Mental—Juvenile literature. [1. Depression, Mental.
2. Suicide. 3. Adolescence. 4. Drug abuse]
I. Title. II. Series.
HV6546.C485   1986   362.2   86-976
ISBN 0-87754-771-8

Chelsea House Publishers

133 Christopher Street, New York, NY 10014

345 Whitney Avenue, New Haven, CT 05510

5014 West Chester Pike, Edgemont, PA 19028

CONTENTS

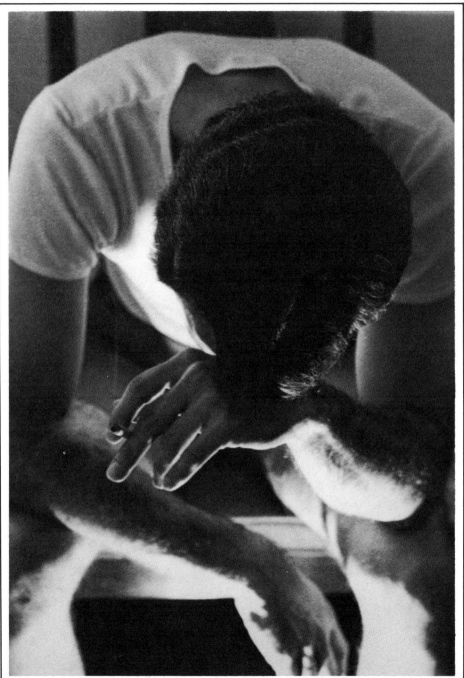

An anguished teenager, cigarette in hand, succumbs to despair. Feelings of hopeless desperation, which can occur at any age but often happen during adolescence, may push a person towards thoughts of suicide.

FOREWORD

In the Mainstream of American Life

The rapid growth of drug use and abuse is one of the most dramatic changes in the fabric of American society in the last 20 years. The United States has the highest level of psychoactive drug use of any industrialized society. It is 10 to 30 times greater than it was 20 years ago.

According to a recent Gallup poll, young people consider drugs the leading problem that they face. One of the legacies of the social upheaval of the 1960s is that psychoactive drugs have become part of the mainstream of American life. Schools, homes, and communities cannot be "drug proofed." There is a demand for drugs—and the supply is plentiful. Social norms have changed and drugs are not only available—they are everywhere.

Almost all drug use begins in the preteen and teenage years. These years are few in the total life cycle, but critical in the maturation process. During these years adolescents face the difficult tasks of discovering their identity, clarifying their sexual roles, asserting their independence, learning to cope with authority, and searching for goals that will give their lives meaning. During this intense period of growth, conflict is inevitable and the temptation to use drugs is great. Drugs are readily available, adolescents are curious and vulnerable, there is peer pressure to experiment, and there is the temptation to escape from conflicts.

No matter what their age or socioeconomic status, no group is immune to the allure and effects of psychoactive drugs. The U.S. Surgeon General's report, "Healthy People," indicates that 30% of all deaths in the United States

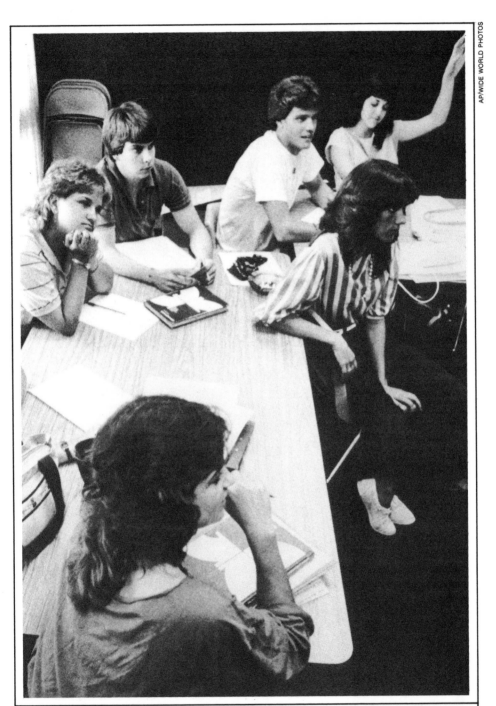

Members of a class designed to help students deal with stress share their experiences. Doctors agree that programs like this one can help prevent normal anxieties from turning into suicidal despair.

are premature because of alcohol and tobacco use. However, the most shocking development in this report is that mortality in the age group between 15 and 24 has increased since 1960 despite the fact that death rates for all other age groups have declined in the 20th century. Accidents, suicides, and homicides are the leading cause of death in young people 15 to 24 years of age. In many cases the deaths are directly related to drug use.

THE ENCYCLOPEDIA OF PSYCHOACTIVE DRUGS answers the questions that young people are likely to ask about drugs, as well as those they might not think to ask, but should. Topics include: what it means to be intoxicated; how drugs affect mood; why people take drugs; who takes them; when they take them; and how much they take. They will learn what happens to a drug when it enters the body. They will learn what it means to get "hooked" and how it happens. They will learn how drugs affect their driving, their schoolwork, and those around them—their peers, their family, their friends, and their employers. They will learn what the signs are that indicate that a friend or a family member may have a drug problem and to identify four stages leading from drug use to drug abuse. Myths about drugs are dispelled.

National surveys indicate that students are eager for information about drugs and that they respond to it. Students not only need information about drugs—they want information. How they get it often proves crucial. Providing young people with accurate knowledge about drugs is one of the most critical aspects.

THE ENCYCLOPEDIA OF PSYCHOACTIVE DRUGS synthesizes the wealth of new information in this field and demystifies this complex and important subject. Each volume in the series is written by an expert in the field. Handsomely illustrated, this multi-volume series is geared for teenage readers. Young people will read these books, share them, talk about them, and make more informed decisions because of them.

Miriam Cohen, Ph.D.
Contributing Editor

A woman comforts an adolescent girl in a moment of emotional crisis. Many suicidal teenagers are extremely self-critical. They feel like failures and lack the self-confidence needed to cope with everyday problems. Holding no hope for the future, they see suicide as a realistic "solution" to the difficulties they are experiencing.

INTRODUCTION

The Gift of Wizardry
Use and Abuse

JACK H. MENDELSON, M.D.
NANCY K. MELLO, PH.D.
Alcohol and Drug Abuse Research Center
Harvard Medical School—McLean Hospital

Dorothy to the Wizard:

"I think you are a very bad man," said Dorothy.
"Oh, no, my dear; I'm really a very good man; but I'm a very bad
Wizard."

—from THE WIZARD OF OZ

Man is endowed with the gift of wizardry, a talent for discovery and invention. The discovery and invention of substances that change the way we feel and behave are among man's special accomplishments, and like so many other products of our wizardry, these substances have the capacity to harm as well as to help. The substance itself is neutral, an intricate molecular structure. Yet, "too much" can be sickening, even deadly. It is man who decides how each substance is used, and it is man's beliefs and perceptions that give this neutral substance the attributes to heal or destroy.

Consider alcohol—available to all and yet regarded with intense ambivalence from biblical times to the present day. The use of alcoholic beverages dates back to our earliest ancestors. Alcohol use and misuse became associated with the worship of gods and demons. One of the most powerful Greek gods was Dionysus, lord of fruitfulness and god of wine. The Romans adopted Dionysus but changed his name to Bacchus. Festivals and holidays associated with Bacchus celebrated the harvest and the origins of life. Time has blurred the images of the Bacchanalian festival, but the theme of drunkenness as a major part of celebration has survived the pagan gods and remains a familiar part of modern society.

13

The term "Bacchanalian festival" conveys a more appealing image than "drunken orgy" or "pot party," but whatever the label, some of the celebrants will inevitably start up the "high" escalator to the next plateau. Once there, the de-escalation is difficult for many.

According to reliable estimates, one out of every ten Americans develops a serious alcohol-related problem sometime in his or her lifetime. In addition, automobile accidents caused by drunken drivers claim the lives of tens of thousands every year. Many of the victims are gifted young people, just starting out in adult life. Hospital emergency rooms abound with patients seeking help for alcohol-related injuries.

Who is to blame? Can we blame the many manufacturers who produce such an amazing variety of alcoholic beverages? Should we blame the educators who fail to explain the perils of intoxication, or so exaggerate the dangers of drinking that no one could possibly believe them? Are friends to blame— those peers who urge others to "drink more and faster," or the macho types who stress the importance of being able to "hold your liquor"? Casting blame, however, is hardly constructive, and pointing the finger is a fruitless way to deal with problems. Alcoholism and drug abuse have few culprits but many victims. Accountability begins with each of us, every time we choose to use or to misuse an intoxicating substance.

It is ironic that some of man's earliest medicines, derived from natural plant products, are used today to poison and to intoxicate. Relief from pain and suffering is one of society's many continuing goals. Over 3,000 years ago, the Therapeutic Papyrus of Thebes, one of our earliest written records, gave instructions for the use of opium in the treatment of pain. Opium, in the form of its major derivative, morphine, remains one of the most powerful drugs we have for pain relief. But opium, morphine, and similar compounds, such as heroin, have also been used by many to induce changes in mood and feeling. Another example of man's misuse of a natural substance is the coca leaf, which for centuries was used by the Indians of Peru to reduce fatigue and hunger. Its modern derivative, cocaine, has important medical use as a local anesthetic. Unfortunately, its increasing abuse in the 1980s has reached epidemic proportions.

The purpose of this series is to provide information about the nature and behavioral effects of alcohol and drugs, and the probable consequences of their use. The information presented here (and in other books in this series) is based on many clinical and laboratory studies and observations by people from diverse walks of life.

Over the centuries, novelists, poets, and dramatists have provided us with many insights into the beneficial and problematic aspects of alcohol and drug use. Physicians, lawyers, biologists, psychologists, and social scientists have contributed to a better understanding of the causes and consequences of using these substances. The authors in this series have attempted to gather and condense all the latest information about drug use and abuse. They have also described the sometimes wide gaps in our knowledge and have suggested some new ways to answer many difficult questions.

One such question, for example, is how do alcohol and drug problems get started? And what is the best way to treat them when they do? Not too many years ago, alcoholics and drug abusers were regarded as evil, immoral, or both. It is now recognized that these persons suffer from very complicated diseases involving complex biological, psychological, and social problems. To understand how the disease begins and progresses, it is necessary to understand the nature of the substance, the behavior and genetic makeup of the afflicted person, and the characteristics of the society or culture in which he lives.

The diagram below shows the interaction of these three factors. The arrows indicate that the substance not only affects the user personally, but the society as well. Society influences attitudes towards the substance, which in turn affect its availability. The substance's impact upon the society may support or discourage the use and abuse of that substance.

SUBSTANCE
(ALCOHOL OR DRUG)

PERSON ⟷ SOCIETY

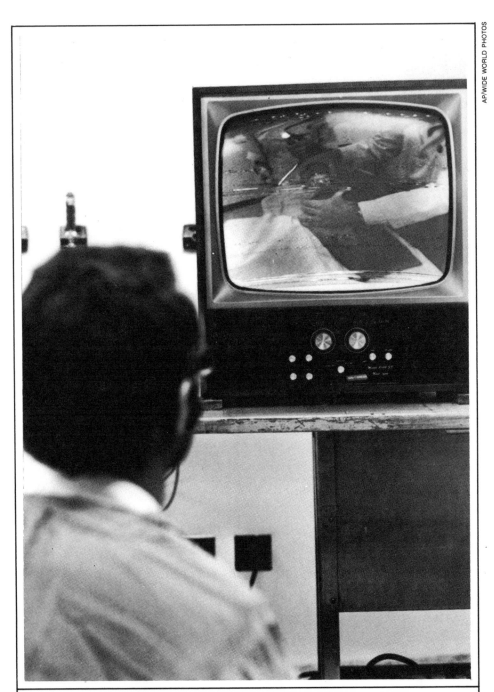

A suicide patient at the National Naval Medical Center in Bethesda, Md., watches a film recording of his own emergency treatment. People who have attempted to take their own lives will sometimes deny that they are suicidal, which can delay treatment of underlying problems.

Although many of the social environments we live in are very similar, some of the most subtle differences can strongly influence our thinking and behavior. Where we live, go to school and work, whom we discuss things with—all influence our opinions about drug use and misuse. Yet we also share certain commonly accepted beliefs that outweigh any differences in our attitudes. The authors in this series have tried to identify and discuss the central, most crucial issues concerning drug use and misuse.

Regrettably, man's wizardry in developing new substances in medical therapeutics has not always been paralleled by intelligent usage. Although we do know a great deal about the effects of alcohol and drugs, we have yet to learn how to impart that knowledge, especially to young adults.

Does it matter? What harm does it do to smoke a little pot or have a few beers? What is it like to be intoxicated? How long does it last? Will it make me feel really fine? Will it make me sick? What are the risks? These are but a few of the questions answered in this series, which, hopefully, will enable the reader to make wise decisions concerning the crucial issue of drugs.

Information sensibly acted upon can go a long way towards helping everyone develop his or her best self. As one keen and sensitive observer, Dr. Lewis Thomas, has said,

> There is nothing at all absurd about the human condition. We matter. It seems to me a good guess, hazarded by a good many people who have thought about it, that we may be engaged in the formation of something like a mind for the life of this planet. If this is so, we are still at the most primitive stage, still fumbling with language and thinking, but infinitely capacitated for the future. Looked at this way, it is remarkable that we've come as far as we have in so short a period, really no time at all as geologists measure time. We are the newest, the youngest, and the brightest thing around.

A boy looks down at the river from his perch on this Pittsburgh bridge. Most people who think of suicide never actually try to kill themselves, and most people who do attempt to take their own lives do not succeed.

CHAPTER 1

THE MANY FACES OF SUICIDAL BEHAVIOR

Mahatma Gandhi, the Indian leader whose name and life have come to symbolize much of what is positive, creative, and beneficial in the human experience, was at the age of 14 suicidal. He later wrote, "Our want of independence began to smart. It was unbearable that we should be unable to do anything without the elders' permission. At last, in sheer disgust, we decided to commit suicide! . . . We heard that Dhatura seeds were an effective poison. Off we went to the jungle in search of these seeds, and got them. . . . But our courage failed us. Supposing we were not instantly killed? And what was the good of killing ourselves? Why not rather put up with the lack of independence? But we swallowed two or three seeds nevertheless. We dared not take more. Both of us fought shy of death, and decided to go to Rama Mandir to compose ourselves and to dismiss the thought of suicide."

Like Gandhi, many teenagers have probably at one point or another contemplated suicide, but in the end they found other ways to cope with life's inevitable problems "shy of death."

This book will explore the interrelatedness of drugs, teenage depression, and suicide. Among 15- to 19-year-olds, suicide is the third leading cause of death, exceeded only by traffic accidents and murders. The suicide rate among 15- to 24-year-olds has nearly tripled in the last 25 years. About 7,000 teenagers kill themselves yearly and many more make the attempt. What is the cause of this dramatic increase? What role do drugs play in the emotional upheavals that teenagers experience in their everyday life? What pressures cause happiness and hope to dissolve into depression and despair? The following will attempt to shed some light on these questions.

Suicidology

For much of the time that suicidal behavior has been studied (a discipline now known as suicidology), researchers have tended to lump together people who think about suicide, those who attempt suicide, and still a third group of persons who actually commit suicide. It was assumed, for example, that studying people who had attempted suicide would lead to new insights and findings about suicide completers, which in turn might reveal ways to prevent suicide. In fact, however, most people who consider suicide never actually attempt to kill themselves, and most people who do attempt to take their own lives do not succeed.

Although this book will explore the characteristics of people in each of these three groups, its emphasis will be on

"I think of killing myself every day. I can't get the thought out of my mind. I think that things would be better if I were dead." Ideas such as these are typical of the thinking of someone who is potentially suicidal.

ART RESOURCE

young people who attempt suicide. The connection between suicide and drug use will also be explored. The principal aim of this book is to help teenagers find ways of dealing with their problems — ways that do not involve suicide or drugs. No one can be sure when or if an individual who is thinking of suicide will make an attempt. Likewise, one can never be certain when a troubled adolescent will impulsively think of suicide and act on that impulse. What we can be sure of, however, is that once the red flag of someone's suicidal tendencies is waved, there are things we can do to help. In fact, our prompt and decisive reaction to such a signal may possibly prevent tragedy.

Contemplating Suicide

About 2,000 years ago, an adolescent boy in China wrote of his life and thoughts about suicide:

> My tears fell and fell
> And I went on sobbing and sobbing.
> In winter I have no great-coat;
> Nor in summer, thin clothes.
> It is no pleasure to be alive.
> I had rather quickly leave the earth
> And go beneath the Yellow Springs.
> The April winds blow
> And the Grass is growing green.
> In the third month — silkworms and mulberries,
> In the sixth month — the melon harvest.
> I went out with the melon-cart
> And just as I was coming home
> The melon-cart turned over.
> The people who came to help me were few,
> But the people who ate the melons were many,
> All they left me were the stalks —
> To take home as fast as I could.
> My brother and sister-in-law were harsh,
> They asked me all sorts of awful questions.
> Why does everyone in the village hate me?
> I want to write a letter and send it
> To my mother and father under the earth,
> And tell them I can't go on any longer
> Living with my brother and sister-in-law.

In our time, a 16-year-old boy who had often thought about suicide wrote:

He always wanted to explain things
But no one cared.
The teacher came and spoke to him.
She told him to wear a tie like all the other boys.
He said it didn't matter.
After that they drew.
And he drew all yellow and it was the way he felt
    about the morning
And it was beautiful.

The teacher came and smiled at him.
"What is this?" she said. "Why don't you draw some-
    thing like Ken is drawing
Isn't that beautiful?"
After that his mother bought him a tie.
And he always drew airplanes and rocket ships like
    everyone else.
And he threw the old picture away.
And when he lay out alone looking at the sky
It was big and blue and all of everything.
But he wasn't anymore.
He was square inside and brown
And his hands were still
And he was like everyone else.
And the things inside him that needed saying didn't
    need it anymore.
It had stopped pushing.
It was crushed.
Stiff
Like everything else.

Both poems painfully illustrate adolescent turmoil, and dramatize the sad reality that for some young people death might somehow be preferable to life. The idea that the teenage years are a time of particular stress and upheaval is a common one. It has even been suggested that adolescents who on the surface seem to be the most normal and well-balanced may, in fact, run the greatest risk of developing problems. But this is a dangerous and unfounded notion. Most adolescents are relatively stable, get along with their peers and parents, and generally have a positive and healthy outlook on life. It is also not true that serious thoughts of suicide afflict teenagers any more than persons in other age categories. Actually, it is among people over the age of 65 that suicidal thinking is most common.

Suicide and Psychiatric Disorders

An adolescent who does entertain serious thoughts of suicide, however, obviously has serious problems. Never should it be assumed that he or she is merely a teenager "passing through a difficult stage." Serious suicidal thoughts are often directly associated with significant psychiatric disorders such as depression, psychosis, and drug addiction, all of which require treatment.

It is difficult to know who will actually attempt suicide, but generally those adolescents who experience hopelessness, helplessness, and alienation are more apt to be self-destructive and to make a suicide attempt. A simple question, "Would any of your problems be solved if you killed your-

UPI/BETTMANN NEWSPHOTOS

This drawing of a hostile boy, which was done by a schizophrenic patient, can be interpreted as an apt depiction of the frustration and anger that is present in many suicidal people.

self?" is a useful part of any discussion with someone considering suicide. A definite "yes" in response should raise immediate warning signs.

Taken from a psychological test known as the Beck Hopelessness Inventory, here are some examples of questions to which a hopeless person would likely answer yes.

> I might as well give up because I can't make things go better for myself.
> I just don't get the breaks, and there is no reason to believe I will in the future.
> All I can see ahead of me is unpleasantness rather than pleasantness.
> I don't expect to get what I really want.
> Things just won't work out the way I want them to.
> I never get what I want so it's foolish to want anything.
> The future seems vague and uncertain to me.

This sense of despair, with its view of the world as a vague, unfriendly place where things usually do not work out, must be looked for, dealt with, and repeatedly checked on in any attempt to help an adolescent who has serious thoughts of suicide.

ART RESOURCE

It should never be assumed that a teenager with suicidal thoughts is merely experiencing "adolescent turmoil" or "passing through a phase."

Who Is Vulnerable?

Thinking about, attempting, and actually committing suicide are, of course, vastly different. For one thing, suicide and suicide attempts rarely occur before the age of 12, but then, and continuing through the teenage years, both increase with age. Also there are many more unsuccessful than completed acts among adolescents. In fact, for every suicide among adolescents there are 100 to 150 attempts. Also, attempted suicides drop off rapidly after age 30, while completed suicides steadily increase with age. Suicide among young people is more common in males, while suicide attempts are far more prevalent among females. Over the last two decades suicide attempts among adolescents have increased more dramatically than suicides. Evidence of a link between those youths who do commit suicide and those who attempt it is scanty. In one 10- to 20-year follow-up study, 10% of male suicide attempters eventually committed suicide, while only 2.9% of females did the same. What we must offer our troubled friends

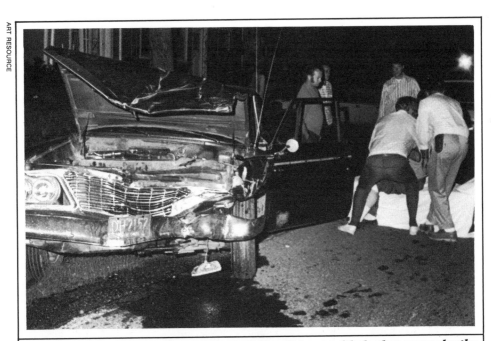

Many suicides do not show up in statistics. It is very likely that some deaths that are the result of "accidents," such as car wrecks, self-poisoning, or gunshot wounds, may actually be suicides.

or family members has more to do with helping them learn nondestructive approaches to their difficulties than with preventing their eventual deaths by suicide.

The suicide rate in the United States for adolescents and young adults rose 131% from 1961 to 1975, and most indications are that it is continuing to increase in the 1980s. For males aged 15 to 24 the rate today is approximately four times as high as it is for females in the same age category. Most reports and surveys indicate that white adolescents run a greater risk of becoming suicide victims than members of other racial groups.

The statistics that show the alarming increase in adolescent suicide probably also underestimate the severity of the problem. Deaths that are possibly suicidal, such as single-car accidents, poisonings, and "accidental" gunshot wounds, may not show up in suicide statistics. Given a choice, many families, and indeed even many medical examiners, would prefer to list a death as the result of an accident rather than a suicide.

The Stigma of Suicide

For centuries, a stigma has been attached to suicide. The Roman Catholic church, for instance, considers it self-murder. Suicide is also frowned on in cultures other than our own.

Ophelia *by J. E. Millais depicts a scene from Shakespeare's* Hamlet. *Works of art have sometimes romanticized the tragic act of suicide.*

Islam forbids suicide as an act against God. In many African and Asian societies, people who have committed suicide are denied burial in sacred ground. In Benin, Africa, the bodies of suicide victims are not allowed ceremonial burials, but are instead thrown into the fields to be devoured by wild animals. In some parts of Cambodia, people who die by their own hands are buried in a remote corner of the forest, far from the graves of their neighbors.

Survivors' Grief

Adolescent suicide, understandably, has a powerful effect on the victim's family and friends, who often have great difficulty accepting it. The immediate family can be especially hard hit. Parents often refuse to accept the death as a suicide, and may show anger at well-intentioned friends trying to help them come to grips with facing the truth. Tremendous guilt, shame, and depression commonly afflict the surviving family members. Also post-suicide grief tends to linger more than that for a normal death, often causing anguish for years.

AP/WIDE WORLD PHOTOS

Classmates register shock and disbelief and the school nurse summons emergency aid after a teenager shoots himself during a high school graduation ceremony in South Weymouth, Massachusetts.

Studies show that stressful events such as broken romances, family tension, problems at school, and other pressures of adolescence are among the factors that can precipitate a suicide attempt.

CHAPTER 2

ADOLESCENT SUICIDE

*I*t is rare for young children to be suicidal. This is not because they do not lead troubled lives or because they do not have emotional or physical problems. Many of them do indeed lead miserable lives and are unhappy. They also live in a world of giants, on whom they are completely dependent. If those giants are indifferent, or worse, cruel, children can easily find themselves in a hopeless and terrifying situation. Yet, they seldom attempt suicide. The reasons for this are complex, and not fully understood. One psychological fact often noted is that children, prior to the age of about eight, do not have a sense of what dying means. Without a real comprehension of what death is, it is probably not possible even to think of suicide. Suicidal behavior first creeps into our statistical tables at around the age of 12 and rises steadily through the teen years and beyond.

The Turbulent Years

One reason for this is that adolescence represents the time that individuals must confront the problems of becoming sexually mature. Since the turn of the century the age at which American children have become sexually functioning adults has become increasingly lower. Eighty years ago, young women began to menstruate, on the average, at the age of 14. Now, menstruation usually begins between the ages of 11 and 12. Sexual maturity is harder to measure in boys, but it also seems to be starting at an earlier age. Many adolescents find themselves moving toward sexual maturity at a time when their thinking remains basically childlike. Certainly most adults continue to regard them as children. As a result, this can be a most difficult period.

In our society, adolescence is generally harder for girls than for boys. This may be a factor in why suicide attempts are more common among young women. Boys have traditionally had more obvious ways to measure their development. Athletics and the mastering of mechanical skills, for

Athletic events such as this basketball game provide a healthy release for the frustrations that often plague adolescence. Unfortunately, such activity has traditionally been more available to boys than girls.

AP/WIDE WORLD PHOTOS

example, are easy ways to build confidence and increase self-esteem. Even more important, a girl, at least in our culture, is apt to judge herself by how much other people seem attracted to her. Am I pretty? Am I popular? Sadly, many young women are left feeling at an early age that if they are not attractive or well liked now, they never will be. The attributes by which they gauge their progress often come more from the reaction of others than from a realistic self-appraisal.

Almost all suicidal adolescents have trouble with personal relationships. Sometimes these problems are based on active conflicts, such as family disputes or fights with other teenagers. Or they may be due to loss: loss of friends and family, loss of hope, loss of confidence that there are people willing to support them in times of need.

Family Conflicts

Family conflict is often the trigger for adolescent suicide attempts. Interactions between parent and teenager in these troubled families are too often based on emotion rather than

Is she pretty? Is she likeable? Is she attractive to men? The self-esteem of adolescent girls is too often based on the judgments of others, and many fear that if they are not popular or attractive now, they never will be.

reason. Moreover, most of the emotional interaction is negative from the point of view of both the parent and the adolescent. Frequent, often daily, quarreling with one or both parents is often a factor in teenage suicide or suicide attempts. Similarly, a suicidal adolescent is often in conflict with a brother or sister or even with an aunt, uncle, or grandparent. Understandably, many suicidal teenagers see this as an impossible and terrible situation. They rely on their family for food, shelter, and the basic needs of life, and yet nearly every encounter with their family is unpleasant and frightening.

Another frequent problem for the suicidal teenager is the broken romance. Adolescence is the time when young people begin to look outside their families toward a life away from home and toward relationships with other people. The early steps towards outside attachments often result in what has been called "puppy love." Adolescents meet one another and become infatuated. They become highly involved in the relationship, which often turns out to be as brief as it is intense.

Separation, *by the well-known Norwegian painter Edvard Munch. Many adolescents who are potentially suicidal have suffered a tragic loss, such as the death of a parent or close friend.*

For some, however, "puppy love" can be a devastating experience. A teenager suddenly finds someone else who seems wonderful in every way. He or she often endows this person with marvelous but unrealistic attributes. He or she can do no wrong. Once the unstable relationship breaks down, however, as it so often does, the results can be disastrous. The ensuing trauma may represent the emotional low point of a teenager's young life. For those prone to suicidal behavior, it is a moment of great risk.

A deep sense of loss is another emotion that can cause teenagers to attempt or commit suicide. Whether it be the loss of a parent through death or divorce, or the loss of a close friend who has moved away, suicidal teenagers are often unable to adapt to this loss or to make and keep a new intimate friend. Instead they tend to become lonely and even further isolated.

An unshakable feeling of failure, deep dejection, a sense that things will not improve — for the suicidal teenager, things are either black or white.

For suicidal adolescents life is usually full of negative emotions: anger, guilt, depression, anxiety, or boredom. When stressful situations arise, as they do for all of us, almost every suicidal adolescent will be plagued by very strong and persistent feelings that these situations are unbearable. To complicate matters, the suicidal teenager often feels guilty about his or her negative feelings, somehow believing that it is wrong to feel so wretched.

Many suicidal adolescents tend to be extremely self-critical. They often see themselves as failures and as having let down their family and friends. They have little faith in their ability to cope with life or its inevitable stresses. They foresee little hope for the future and have almost no sense of the gray areas of life. For them, most things are all or nothing, black or white, right or wrong. In other words, their thinking often seems locked in concrete. When asked to try to imagine new ways of thinking about things, suicidal teenagers will often reply, "Why? Things just are the way they are and cannot change." The fact that adolescents who are suicidal rarely consider the long-term effects of their actions often prevents them from realizing the destructive results of their actions.

Almost all suicidal teenagers will agree with the statement, "Suicide is an effective solution to life's problems." Somehow, they have developed the notion that it is a realistic alternative to coping with their difficulties. They are often convinced that actions speak louder than words, that "doing something" about a bad situation might help, while "talking it through" never does. In fact, many of them think that talking things over will only make matters worse.

Eating Disorders and Suicide

The association of alcohol and suicidal behavior has been thoroughly studied. Up to one-half of all suicide attempters have been drinking at the time of their attempt. As noted earlier, there is now much clinical evidence to implicate other drugs of abuse as well. In addition, bulimia, an eating disorder in which an individual periodically gorges him or herself with food in order to relieve a bad feeling, has recently been identified as a problem for many teenagers, especially young women. There are now some indications that bulimia, with or without changes in weight, is associated with a greater risk for suicidal behavior. Eating disorders, drug abuse, and suicidal behavior are all often impulsive and destructive acts undertaken to change a situation and/or relieve a bad feeling. In this regard, it can be useful to think of suicidal behavior as addictive behavior, and indeed, it does follow some of the models of addiction. It is almost always preceded by a buildup of tension and anxiety. Like drug abuse and bulimia, a suicide attempt seems to relieve that tension and anxiety. Often, adolescents who make a suicide attempt state that they feel better afterwards. The negative consequences of the suicide attempt, just like the negative effects of drug abuse and bulimia, are less readily apparent and often not nearly as important to the adolescent as the tension relief they provide. They do something, and it makes them feel better. Unfortunately, this often leads to the action being repeated.

Jane Fonda, one of the most famous actresses in contemporary society, struggled against bulimia as a young woman. This eating disorder, in which compulsive overeating is followed by vomiting, is associated with an increased risk of suicidal behavior.

Sally: A Case Study

To sum up many of the aspects of adolescent suicide let us look at the case of a young woman we shall call Sally.

She came from a troubled family. She was the youngest of four children and the only daughter. Her parents had married when they were young — her mother was 15 and her father 18. At the time of the marriage the mother had been pregnant. Sally's father, although alcoholic, was hard working and had started a successful small business. By the time he was 30, however, his alcoholism markedly interfered with his business and family life. He sexually assaulted his sons, and was ordered by a court to undergo psychological treatment. Between the ages of 6 and 9, Sally was sexually molested by her brothers on numerous occasions. When she was 9, her father died. It was a heavy blow. She had been her father's "favorite." The mother carried on the family business and did surprisingly well. Sally did not fare so well. As a young child she had been successful in school. Now she began to feel increasingly lonely and isolated, and her schoolwork suffered. More and more she withdrew to her room, although her actions were largely ignored by the rest of the family. Her mother, discussing the events later, remembers being preoccupied at the time with the older brothers' drinking and being grateful that Sally caused her no trouble.

By the time she was 13, Sally had become an attractive young woman. She began to go out, usually with men much older than herself. She began to drink, to use marijuana, and later to use cocaine. Her mother became furious with her, and the two began to have daily arguments. Sally was portrayed as destroying the family happiness. Her brothers even beat up one of her boyfriends. Sally's response to that was to find an older, stronger boyfriend of whom her brothers were afraid. The family did make some attempt to talk out their differences but Sally saw the discussions as unrealistic and unrewarding. To her, drugs and parties were the only things that kept her from being totally depressed. At one point she did make a move to leave her boyfriend. Ironically, her mother chose the occasion to accuse her of being disloyal to him. The family actually seemed threatened by Sally's step toward self-improvement. Increasingly, her mother and brothers told Sally that life would be better for all if she would just "go away." Then, when Sally was 16, her boyfriend was imprisoned. Sally was devastated. One afternoon, she began drinking her mother's whiskey — something she had been forbidden to do. After drinking about half a bottle, she impulsively went to the medicine chest and swallowed all of the pills in a bottle of antidepressant medication that had been prescribed for her mother. She passed out. The dose she had taken was potentially lethal. Luckily, one of her brothers soon found her, figured out what had happened, and got her to the hospital. After medical treatment, Sally began a long — and eventually successful — period of therapy, in which her family was to play an important part.

Specially trained police officers gently persuade a troubled teenager to abandon her perch on New York's Brooklyn Bridge. One recent study indicates that up to one-half of all those who attempt suicide have been drinking at the time of their attempt.

A funeral service is held for a high school student, one of the victims of a rash of suicides among Texas teenagers. Studies show that most drug-abusing, suicidal adolescents come from profoundly unstable living situations characterized by insecurity, anger, and hostility.

CHAPTER 3

FAMILIES AND SUICIDE

*P*rofessionals working with suicidal, drug-abusing teenagers have studied their families in detail. Many of the families have chronic difficulties. Not surprisingly, such young people do not, as a rule, spring abruptly from previously untroubled homes. They are much more likely to come from unstable, unstructured living situations that are characterized by hostility, insecurity, and antisocial conduct. In such an environment, actions are more important than words, and impulsive behavior is the general rule. For such families, life is a constant state of stress, in which marital difficulties, economic woes, and alcohol and drug abuse are commonplace. In many troubled families, members seem to live from day to day, with little concern for the past or future. There is usually not much affection or warmth, and the parents often have mixed feelings about their children. Indeed, they may even resent having had them in the first place and often appear overwhelmed by parental responsibilities. At times, they are emotionally cold and distant, at other times critical and angry. As a result, children in such families learn at an early age to "lie low." They learn that it is better not to be seen or heard, and especially not to ask for help. When the need for emotional contact with their parents becomes overwhelming, they often resort to dramatic action to get attention.

Fixed Roles

Families with a drug abusing and suicidal teenager often demonstrate a rigid style, in which family members are locked into fixed roles, whether they like that role or not. In such families one role is often that of the scapegoat. This is often the teenager who gets blamed whenever anything goes wrong. Other family members, of course, usually deny placing the blame on the "goat." They deny the truth of Mark Twain's observation, "Town drunk is an elected office."

Another fixed role in such families is that of the "parentified" child. This is the youngster who has to look after

Divorce, desertion, separation. Drug-abusing and suicidal teenagers often feel abandoned by parents who are themselves suffering from severe personal problems.

ART RESOURCE

one or both parents, worrying about them, and spending a great deal of energy on the parents' needs rather than his or her own.

Adolescents in these fixed roles feel trapped and unable to change. While both parents and teenagers may complain bitterly about the way things are, they will often tenaciously resist any attempt to change the status quo. During adolescence it is natural for a person to try many different roles, to see which fits best. If this desire is blocked and only one role — and usually an unwanted one — is permitted, a child may seek other ways to escape. Unfortunately, this can be a route to drug use and suicidal behavior.

Suicidal adolescents often have a fight with one or both parents just prior to attempting suicide. In fact, frequent fighting is much more common in the homes of suicidal adolescents than in the homes of troubled but not suicidal youngsters.

In the 1981 film Ordinary People, *Mary Tyler Moore played the mother of a suicidal son, portrayed by Timothy Hutton. As this movie dramatizes, teenagers in troubled families who are used as emotional scapegoats can become depressed and enraged to the point of suicide.*

A Lack of Communication

Another characteristic of families of drug-abusing and suicidal adolescents frequently noted by mental health workers is a lack of communication within these families. This has been demonstrated both experimentally and by observation. The family seems to have little ability to organize itself to work toward common goals. The gift of language has little problem-solving value to such a family. Ironically, the parents and children will often ally themselves against outside intervention and help. School counselors often grow frustrated with parents who frequently complain about their children but quickly become angry when "authorities" attempt to introduce some positive change. Such persons somehow feel less threatened by a painful status quo than by the prospect of coming to terms with their problems.

SCALA/ART RESOURCE

Eleven A.M., *a painting by Edward Hopper, vividly captures a mood of desolation. Adolescents can be driven to thoughts of suicide by the loneliness that results from a lack of communication within a family.*

The Hereditary Factor

It should also be mentioned that some psychiatric illnesses run in families. Depression, anxiety disorders, alcoholism, and antisocial personality are among them. If one person in a family suffers from one of these disorders, the odds are increased that another member has, or may develop, the same disorder. But if that person is identified, he or she might well benefit from treatment.

When a family has to face the fact that one of its children has committed suicide, that realization is likely to produce reactions of anger, guilt, and shame as well as the normal sorrow. Moreover, the grief will tend to linger, creating new problems for what may be an already troubled family. Some families will not be able to cope with this situation and many mental health workers feel that such families need assistance

ART RESOURCE

A mother and daughter embrace. The family that can provide communication, love, and support for its members is, in the cultural critic Christopher Lasch's phrase, "a haven in a heartless world."

to help them become less defensive and more flexible. This effort has been called *postvention*, in contrast to *prevention*, and can be provided by health professionals, teachers, religious figures or even by friends. It is important that the offer of help be made quickly, preferably within 24 hours of the suicide. Many survivors will be shocked and emotionally numb during this time and warm and caring support can help set the family's grief on a natural course and prevent it from turning into anger and bitterness. In some American cities aid groups for families of suicide victims have been formed for just this purpose.

One Family's Tragedy

Andrew hanged himself at the age of 17. He was the third of five children and his father was an alcoholic. An older sister had previously made several suicide attempts. Andrew himself had abused several different drugs. A year before his death, he had dropped out of school. He had become increasingly solitary and uncommunicative. On the day of his death he had been drinking alone and the coroner later reported that the level of alcohol in his blood indicated he was intoxicated. He left no suicide note.

At the time of Andrew's death, his mother was being treated by a psychiatrist for depression. She had spoken often of her family's troubles, but had been unable to persuade any of them to join her in seeking treatment. The other family members also rejected the physician's request for an interview to discuss their problems and to get ideas on what should be done.

But three days after Andrew's death, the psychiatrist was able to arrange to visit the family's home. Both parents and the two younger sons were present. The mother was distraught. The rest of the family seemed numb and unable to comfort her.

Much of the conversation focused on helping the family members express their feelings. The father and sons were encouraged not to be embarrassed by the behavior of Andrew's mother. Instead, they were encouraged to share her sadness. The absent older daughter was discussed. The doctor tried to explore the possibility that she, too, felt very bad about the death, and perhaps even blamed herself for it. Her father however, said she was callous and was someone "who cares nothing for the family." The physician stressed that at such times a family needed friends and he made several calls to relatives to enlist their support.

Over the next three months there were four similar family meetings. They most frequently discussed the guilt the family felt about not paying attention to Andrew's depression and isolation, clues he had given them about being suicidal. The mother continued to exhibit the deepest grief. In the fourth session, the psychiatrist emphasized the point that there was something to be learned from Andrew's death, that his problems were shared by the entire family.

A follow-up session was held close to the first anniversary of Andrew's death. Both sons were stable emotionally and the father had somewhat curtailed his drinking. The mother's chronic depression however, continued. The oldest daughter, who had come to just one of the sessions, had left home. She was no longer speaking to the family, and had recently tried again to commit suicide.

AP/WIDE WORLD PHOTOS

This task force of doctors was unable to find reasons for the epidemic of suicides in an affluent Texas suburb. Despite extensive research, no one can predict with absolute certainty who will commit suicide.

"Sensitive as a burn." This phrase, from a novel by Isaac Rosenfeld, reflects the emotional vulnerability that can drive a disturbed teenager to drugs, and sometimes even to thoughts of suicide.

CHAPTER 4

DRUGS AND SUICIDE

Drugs can kill those who abuse them in three general ways: by overdose, through side effects or bad reactions, and as a means of committing suicide.

Sometimes, however, drug-related deaths do not fit neatly into any of these categories. Many deaths involving barbiturates, for example, have been ruled accidental on the assumption that the victim's memory had become so clouded by the drug that the victim had simply lost track of the number of pills being taken.

Narcotics addicts, as well, have been known to die after using a drug that their bodies had previously tolerated.

Some drugs may cause both murderous and suicidal behavior. The hallucinogens, especially PCP, are infamous in this respect. Valium has also been cited as producing unwanted suicidal thoughts in some people. Drugs that affect mood and lessen self-control can lead to a lack of restraint that promotes suicidal behavior. In this way, many people who drink to excess become both depressed and reckless.

Of course, many people who use drugs will not become suicidal. However, the odds that a user will commit suicide rise with the degree of his or her drug abuse. Various studies have pointed out that the rates for both suicide and suicide attempts are between 5 and 20 times higher for drug abusers than for the general population.

Chronic Suicide

Years ago the famous psychiatrist Karl Menninger called alcoholism *chronic suicide*. He believed that the kind of thinking and behavior that produces alcoholism is quite similar to the thinking and behavior that produces suicide. The end result — death — merely takes longer. Abusing any drug is obviously harmful. The only reason for doing so is to satisfy a self-destructive impulse. For this reason many studies link the psychological and emotional characteristics of drug abusers with those of suicidal people. Depression, hopelessness, and a negative attitude toward life are common in both groups. It might be said that drug abusers are on a slow but relentless downhill slide, while people committing suicide have chosen simply to jump off a cliff.

According to the noted psychiatrist Karl Menninger, the thinking and behavior that produce alcoholism are remarkably similar to those which precipitate suicide. Alcoholism, says Dr. Menninger, is a kind of "chronic suicide."

THE BETTMANN ARCHIVE

Which Comes First?

Sometimes, however, it is difficult to decide which came first: drug abuse or the psychological factors that led to it. It may be that when a drug abuser feels depressed and hopeless, it is because he or she is already in the grip of a drug. Very little is known about why some adolescents, and not others, start abusing drugs in the first place. Two teenagers can have similar backgrounds, environments, and emotional states and yet follow very different life paths.

Another much-debated theory is one that holds that drug abuse itself causes suicidal behavior. To get a better understanding of this suggestion, it is necessary first to examine the direct effect of drug abuse on the mind and the body, and second, to explore the effects of drug abuse on personal and social attitudes.

Alcohol and barbiturates are perhaps the two drugs that have been most studied as far as abuse is concerned. Their

This painting by a 38-year-old schizophrenic captures the kind of skewed and distorted view of reality often induced by chronic drug abuse.

UPI/BETTMANN NEWSPHOTOS

excessive use can cause confusion and depression, states of mind conducive to suicide. They can also produce a recklessness that can further produce suicidal behavior. Also they are poisons. The more a person takes in a short period of time, the more likely that person is to die.

Most other drugs that are commonly abused show some or all of the same characteristics. Some of them, such as PCP and Valium, may have the capacity to throw a destructive switch in the brain, leading to murderous or suicidal actions.

Sometimes drug abuse can help bring on depression, and as a result trigger suicidal tendencies. When drug abusers lose interest in their health and hygiene, and their ability to work crumbles, they can become depressed, and may feel hopeless, or even suicidal. To make matters worse, many abusers alienate their family and friends, the very people who might best help them in a crisis.

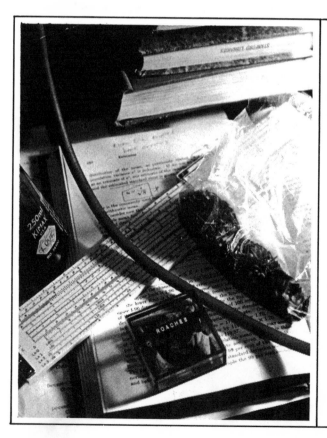

The link between drug and alcohol abuse and suicide has been firmly established: suicide is often the ultimate consequence of addictive behavior.

ART RESOURCE

Suicide and Stress

Suicidal behavior and drug abuse are often associated with another factor: the view that life is a sea of troubles from which suicide and drugs represent a means of escape. For this reason, most instances of overdosing are preceded by periods of stress.

One study showed that people attempting suicide, compared with other groups, experience as many as four times the number of negative events in the six months preceding their attempts to kill themselves. These negative events include illness, the death of a loved one, or legal, school, and job problems. Adolescents attempting suicide frequently note continuous quarrels with one or both of their parents as a major problem in their lives. In addition, many of these youngsters come from troubled or broken homes. The parents themselves abuse drugs or alcohol and they may suffer from depression and other psychiatric disorders or be in trouble at work or with the law. Significantly, the parents may have difficulty in knowing how to relate to others. Other relationships can cause difficulties too. Many suicidal teenagers say that breaking up with a boyfriend or girlfriend leads to their attempt.

This antidrug billboard produced by Rap, Inc. makes an unmistakable equation: angel dust, or PCP, equals suicide.

Anomie

At the turn of the century the French sociologist Émile Durkheim developed a theory that suicide and many other social ills frequently grew out of two broad social characteristics. First, Durkheim felt that every society developed a set of rules regarding behavior that provided guidance to each social member. Too little guidance and too much alienation on the part of the individual — Durkheim called this *anomie* — increase the risk of suicide. Second, Durkheim felt that every society should support, physically and emotionally, its individual members. He showed how all individuals acting together in a society affect the behavior of each and every individual member — Durkheim called this *collective representation*. Too little support from society, or social isolation, can only increase the risk of suicide. Durkheim also advanced the view that to remain stable, society must have a system of common values. Over the years, further work on Durkheim's theory has linked anomie to various antisocial actions, including drug abuse. By observing adolescents afflicted by suicidal behavior or prone to drug abuse, many social scientists have concluded that the two problems are reactions to the same difficulties.

Personality Disorders

The "sea of troubles" idea can cover certain psychiatric illnesses. Schizophrenia, depression, and panic disorder can be associated with drug abuse and/or suicidal behavior. Some people have a type of personality that naturally gets them into trouble with others. While there is a continuing argument about whether or not *personality disorders* are true psychiatric illnesses, it does seem that some are frequently associated with drug abuse or suicidal behavior. It may be that people suffering from one or more of these conditions see drug abuse and suicide as ways out of their troubles.

Personality traits reflect the way individuals look at, relate to, and think about themselves and their environment. When these traits are inflexible, when they prevent someone from relating to others, when they lead to trouble at work or school, or when they cause great distress, they are called personality disorders. They are usually recognizable by the teenage years, but, if untreated, will persist throughout adulthood. Many such disorders have been associated with an increased likelihood of suicidal behavior.

There are arguments for and against each of these theories. But the "sea of troubles" argument seems to explain what we know of some drug-abusing, suicidal teenagers. There probably is more suicidal behavior among adolescents where there is little guidance and much isolation. Crime, family troubles, psychiatric disorders, poverty, and alcohol and drug abuse are frequent factors in the backgrounds of suicidal teenagers.

None of these theories, however, explains the relationship of drugs and suicide. There are many troubled adolescents for whom none of these ideas seems pertinent. Some teenagers fit in with one theory or another very well. Some fit in with all three. Some do not fit any. But we do know that suicidal behavior is much more common among drug abusers than in the general population, and that there are psychological similarities between drug abusers and teenagers who try to commit suicide.

THE BETTMANN ARCHIVE

Emile Durkheim, one of the founders of modern sociology, held that common values are the bonds of social order, and that the loss of such values leads to social and individual instability, as well as to suicidal behavior.

Style of dress or music can reflect the feelings of young people who want to express discontent with their lives. Some people are concerned about lyrics in rock music that glamorize self-destructive behavior.

CHAPTER 5

ASSESSING SUICIDAL BEHAVIOR

*H*ow do you know if some one is suicidal? If such is the case what sort of help is required? What can you do to help?

There is one first step in dealing with all these questions. If you are worried about someone, you should talk with him or her directly about your concerns. This may sound obvious, but to some people it is not that simple. Many people are wary about discussing suicide. They are unsure what to ask and they fear that they will do more harm than good.

Some Myths About Suicide

Several myths surround suicide that prevent people from being more helpful to a potentially suicidal adolescent.

The most common myth is that asking someone about thoughts of suicide may actually cause that person to kill himself or herself. This is simply not true. Individuals thinking of suicide are almost always relieved that someone noticed that something is wrong and is offering to help. They are not made to feel better by being ignored, isolated, and neglected. Talking things over does help.

A second myth is that any person who thinks about suicide is automatically a suicide risk. Many people think about suicide. Far fewer attempt it, and very few actually succeed. A person who persistently thinks about suicide is someone with troubles, but that person is usually not a "suicide risk."

A third myth is that thinking about suicide represents a "bad feeling." Being suicidal is not an emotional state. It is best thought of as a way of dealing with a problem. Suicidal statements or actions, especially when made or done by an adolescent, are often attempts to cope with problems. For example, the parents of a 14-year-old girl were always fighting, especially in the evenings after they had had a few drinks. At first they would argue and insult each other but gradually they would start fighting physically. At this point the girl would leave the house and go to a friend's house. She would tell the friend that she felt "terrible." This friend would call the parents and occasionally the local Crisis Center. Each time the scenario was repeated, the parents would stop fighting. The girl's suicide threats, although they did cause trouble, also brought some stability to the family. Although the 14-year-old described her suicidal tendencies as a "feeling," her actions were clearly a response to a problem.

Is it possible to predict whether someone will commit suicide? Many people assume that it is and expect counselors and therapists to be able to spot a potential suicide victim. However, as two case histories indicate, it is impossible to make this prediction.

Take the case of a young man, an abuser of Angel Dust, whose parents had convinced him to get psychiatric help. After seeing the psychiatrist — call him Dr. Jones — he

Shocking the entire country, six teenagers took their own lives in the small town of Plano, Texas, in 1983. All of the deaths occurred during a six-month period. Four of the victims are pictured on these two pages.

seemed better. His performance at school improved and his relationship with his family was more stable. But after a spat with his girlfriend, he jumped off an eight-story building. Neither Dr. Jones nor his family had suspected he was suicidal.

Dr. Jones had a second patient, a young woman who came from a family in which both her mother and her mother's mother had committed suicide. The young woman suffered periods of severe despondency and sought relief in heavy drug use and sexual promiscuity. Her school work deteriorated, and she was expelled from high school because of truancy and rule breaking. She had constant thoughts of suicide. Although these thoughts stayed with her for over three years and through many crises, she never attempted to kill herself. By the time she was 21, she had managed to graduate from high school, find a fulfilling job, and become happily engaged. She felt that her depression was an illness that she understood and could control. Her drinking and use of drugs had stopped.

In mid-adolescence, suicide had seemed an almost certain part of this young woman's destiny. It never happened.

Although experts cannot explain why, in recent years instances of multiple suicides among adolescents have increased in the United States. Mental health care professionals are mobilizing to fight this epidemic.

Talking About Suicide

It is often erroneously believed that those who talk about suicide are not likely to commit it. While there is some truth to this, most people who persistently talk about suicide *are* in psychological trouble. While a few may make suicide attempts, a very small number will be successful. For this reason it is important to realize from such talk that the person needs help. Therefore, whenever anyone talks about suicide, it is wise to ask, "What problems are you having?"

Barbara: A Case Study

Professionals in such situations seek to discover a number of specific things. Here is how they might conduct an interview. A 16-year-old girl has just taken an overdose of her mother's antidepressant medication. After two days in the hospital she has almost recovered from the effects of the drug. She is about to be interviewed by a doctor, whom we will call Dr. Smith.

The most important part of such an interview is usually the first two or three minutes. An interview that begins badly will probably be unproductive. Vital information may not get discussed, and the problems may not be adequately understood. Individuals who are suicidal usually do not expect help and, as we have seen, have little faith that talking things over will help. Also, many will be angry at the suggestion that there is something mentally or emotionally wrong with them. This makes it crucial that the interviewer is positive, helpful, and able to listen.

Dr. Smith introduces himself to the patient — call her Barbara. He states his reason for being there: He is a psychiatrist. He has been told about Barbara's suicide attempt. He is offering his help.

At first Barbara is reluctant to talk. But the doctor assures her that the interview does not imply a future commitment on her part and that at the end of the interview the two of them will be in a much better position to decide jointly if further talks will be helpful.

Sometimes, despite reassurance and friendliness on the part of the interviewer, people are not willing to discuss problems. When this happens, it is important for the professional to get as much information as possible. Other people can be interviewed and facts about the patient's surroundings, mood, and behavior can be obtained from them. Many states have laws that allow for the hospitalization of individuals, even if they do not consent, if they are considered dangerous to themselves or others. A professional dealing with a suicidal patient should know these laws and the procedures for dealing with them.

In this case, Barbara did begin to talk. Dr. Smith at-first tried to establish her motivation. "Please tell me what happened the day or two before you made your suicide attempt," he asked. He listened patiently as she recounted the events. Twice she digressed to talk about her mother's problems. Each time, Dr. Smith assured her they would have ample time to discuss her mother but that at this point it was important to understand exactly what happened to her, Barbara. At the end of Barbara's account, Dr. Smith had a good idea of what had transpired during the previous 48 hours. He discovered that Barbara had not gone to school on those two days but had stayed in her room. He found out that she had had several intense fights with her mother over Barbara's boyfriend. He learned that Barbara had gone through periods of tension and anxiety and that she had felt a buildup of the feeling that she "just could not stand it any longer." He also discovered that she had been drinking and quite suddenly decided "to end it all." She then had gone to her mother's room and had taken the medication.

A California family mourns the death of their eldest son, who, when denied the use of the family television set, shot and killed himself.

Dr. Smith next wanted to know whether the attempt was impulsive or planned. If it had been planned, he wanted to know how long the plans had been in the making. In Barbara's case, although she had thought about suicide for a long time, she took the overdose within 10 minutes of thinking about doing it. Dr. Smith also wanted to know if Barbara had been alone when she took the drugs or whether someone else was in the room or close by. In other words, was it likely that Barbara would be found soon after the attempt (thus more or less insuring that she would survive) or had she taken precautions to keep from being discovered? The doctor wanted to know what drugs had been taken, in what quantity, and whether or not all the drugs available had been swallowed. He wanted to know what effect Barbara had thought the drugs might have. He asked if she had left any message or note or made any effort to get help after taking the drug. All this information enabled him to estimate how determined Barbara had been about trying to commit suicide. Many doctors feel that understanding a person's suicide intent is the most important factor in predicting future suicidal behavior.

Edward Hopper's Summer in the City *powerfully evokes a sense of depression, which can be a contagious psychological affliction.*

Once Dr. Smith felt he had made a reasonable assessment of Barbara's suicide intent, he tried to find out the reasons for the attempt. He started by asking, "Can you explain why you took the tablets? What were the problems that, in the end, led you to make this suicide attempt?" Later he asked, "What have been the reactions of the other people in your life since this attempt? Have you been surprised at their reactions? What effect did you think your overdose would have on them?" From Barbara's responses, he also learned that Barbara had slit her wrists two years earlier and that the circumstances preceding that attempt had been somewhat similar to the present ones. When asked about what happened after the previous attempt, Barbara told him that for several months afterward the tension between her and her mother had ceased.

The next step in the interview centered on Barbara's current problems: school, family, boyfriend, drug and alcohol use, and unpleasant emotional states. Some were interrelated. For example, she sometimes felt caught between her mother and boyfriend. As the problems were discussed further, more of Barbara's background and previous experiences came to the surface.

A family sits in front of their home on an Oregon Indian reservation. Poverty and hopelessness are epidemic among many Native Americans.

AP/WIDE WORLD PHOTOS

Next, the doctor went through a mental checklist of problems encountered by many people: difficulties with family, boyfriends, or girlfriends; problems with work or school; money problems, trouble with the law; housing troubles; health problems; difficulties with friends; problems of loss or grief; sex problems; problems with drugs or alcohol; and psychiatric problems.

Too much drinking and/or excessive drug use are frequent problems among teenagers who attempt suicide. However, some adolescents are reluctant to talk about alcohol or drugs and the effects these substances may have.

Measuring Substance Abuse

After Dr. Smith found out that Barbara had been drinking at the time of her suicide attempt he tried to establish if alcohol had been a long-term problem for her. He asked some questions to help determine this:

In the 1978 film **The Deer Hunter,** Robert De Niro portrayed a Vietnam prisoner of war who must readjust to civilian life after he returns to the United States. The plight De Niro's character faced in the movie has been a depressing reality for many returning veterans.

AP/WIDE WORLD PHOTOS

Did you ever feel that you had to have a drink or take drugs in order to help you overcome bad feelings or to steady your nerves?

Did you feel that you should cut down on your drinking or drug use?

Did you ever feel guilty about using drugs or drinking?

Have you ever been criticized because of your drinking or drug use, or felt that it annoyed other people?

Is drinking or drug use interfering with your school work?

Is drinking or drug use affecting your reputation?

Do you resent the advice of others who try to get you to stop drinking and/or taking drugs?

Does drinking and/or drug use cause you to have difficulty in sleeping?

Have you ever felt guilty about your drinking?

Do you drink to build up your confidence?

Do you drink or take drugs alone?

Barbara answered yes to most of the questions, giving the doctor fairly strong evidence that drugs and alcohol did indeed present a long-term problem for her.

Why do some adolescents and not others start to abuse alcohol or drugs in the first place? There is evidence that many teenagers who attempt suicide have drinking or drug problems as well.

Depression is perhaps the most common psychiatric disorder associated with suicidal behavior. It is important, however, to remember that many suicidal people are not depressed. On the other hand, the more seriously one thinks about suicide, the more likely he or she is to have a serious depression. There is some evidence, moreover, that when people are both depressed and delusional, they run a high risk for committing suicide. Recently, *anxiety disorders* have been associated with both suicide attempts and completed suicide. Panic disorder is a condition in which someone becomes quite fearful in situations that would ordinarily not be frightening. This terrifying experience seems to arise from nowhere and is often characterized by rapid heartbeat, sweating, shaking, and sometimes even fear of death. These attacks can start in the teenage years and, when untreated, may well steer a person toward contemplating suicide.

After Barbara and Dr. Smith had discussed her problems, they made a quick survey of her life and surroundings. What supportive relationships did she have? To whom did she turn in times of trouble? Did she have a close friend, someone she could discuss her problems with? Was there more than one such friend? How helpful did she feel her immediate family was? Were there any other relatives — grandparents, aunts or uncles — who might be helpful?

Drawing on Personal Resources

The next area explored was Barbara's personal resources. What was she good at? What kind of situations did she feel she could handle? Did she have any confidence in herself? Did she feel that she had strengths and assets that could be developed? How best did she think she could counter her present difficulties?

Dr. Smith also asked about the past. How had she coped with family and school problems? How had family members coped? It was important for Dr. Smith to assess whether Barbara felt she was handling things in her usual way, or not as well as she had done in the past.

Then the doctor asked Barbara to sum up her current problems. He asked her to list three or four matters that were causing her the most trouble. By doing so he was able to break down her general state of crisis into specific areas that could be tackled one at a time.

In the final stage of this assessment, Dr. Smith tried to establish what further help Barbara needed. He had several important decisions to make. Could Barbara take responsibility for herself or would she need a firm hand to guide her, at least temporarily? Did she have a psychiatric illness requiring treatment? Would she accept counseling?

The best way to end an assessment interview is to agree to a contract. This outlines the specific problems to be worked on, and in what order they will be dealt with. It should also be settled whether or not other people, such as family, will be involved. In Barbara's case, she agreed to 10 counseling sessions, three of them with family members present. She and Dr. Smith also agreed to discuss, at the end of the tenth session, what further actions might be helpful.

THE BETTMANN ARCHIVE

The Scream, *by Edvard Munch. For suicidal and drug-abusing teenagers, anxiety can reach levels of intolerable intensity. Relaxation training, meditation, or therapy can help to moderate the severity of these attacks.*

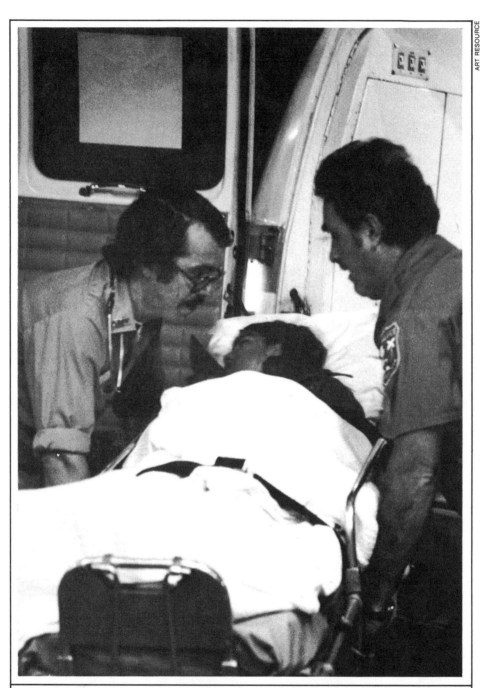

Two paramedics lift an unconscious patient who has attempted suicide into a waiting ambulance. Suicidality is best thought of as an inappropriate way of dealing with a personal problem. If someone talks about suicide, ask, "What problems are you having?"

CHAPTER 6

HELPING SOMEONE WHO HAS OVERDOSED

*T*ragically, many suicide victims are discovered in time for effective treatment but fail to receive it.

Jane, an 18-year-old depressed cocaine addict, took an overdose of the antidepressant drug imipramine. Friends found her four hours later. She was shaky but awake. She seemed in no real danger and begged not to be taken to the hospital for fear that her family would find out what she had done. She swore that she was not suicidal and promised not to overdose again. Her friends, unwisely, consented. Five hours later she was dead. Her heart had suddenly stopped, a well-known effect of an overdose of imipramine.

Treatment Outcome

Some drugs, such as barbiturates, can shut down the brain, including its ability to regulate breathing. Other drugs, such as many antidepressants, not only affect consciousness but can have a direct and fatal effect on the heart.

The amount of the drug taken is obviously important, as is its purity. Street drugs are usually diluted by being mixed with inert substances and so deliver much less actual drug than the volume might suggest. However, some unscrupulous dealers can cut the drug with substances that can be harmful or even fatal. For example, there have been reports of street drugs mixed with rat poison (Coumadin) and strychnine.

In addition to the nature of the drug and the amount taken, a victim's state following an overdose will be affected by the length of time that has passed. In addition, tolerance of a drug can vary from person to person. Habitual narcotics users can tolerate much larger doses of drugs than someone who is not accustomed to using them. And, if other substances are taken with the drug used in an overdose, that too can affect the outcome.

Alcohol is frequently used by someone preparing for an overdose. And it almost always makes more deadly the effects of the other drug.

Lastly, someone who has taken an overdose may have other medical or psychiatric problems. These too can have a powerful influence on the success or failure of treatment.

Alcohol intensifies the effects of other drugs, increasing their lethal potential. For this reason, a combination of alcohol and other depressant drugs is often chosen by those wishing to commit suicide.

ART RESOURCE

Call for Help

The first thing to do after finding someone who has obviously taken an overdose is to call for help. It is a mistake to try to judge whether or not the victim is likely to recover unaided. Most people simply do not have the information, the experience, or the knowledge to make such a vital judgment. A qualified medical evaluation is essential.

If the victim is conscious, it can be assumed that he or she is in a state of emotional distress. It is important to realize this when trying to help.

In providing help, there are four steps that can be taken while waiting for the medical help to arrive. First, it is important to be supportive. Look and sound concerned and

Many suicidal people feel lost, alone, and frightened; often they sense that their current feelings of gloom are not temporary but are instead a permanent state of mind.

UPI/BETTMANN NEWSPHOTOS

caring, but avoid seeming frightened or tense. Make eye contact. Speak in a reassuring tone and have a reassuring touch when that is appropriate.

Second, orient the victim. For example, the conversation can be as simple as this: "Bob, it's Joe. It's about 2 o'clock in the morning. You've taken an overdose. We're in the kitchen of your house. I'm doing my best to see you get help. I've called for an ambulance. And now I'm going to ask you some questions to find out more about what has happened."

Third, communicate clearly and simply. Someone in a diminished state of consciousness will have a better chance of understanding you if you speak slowly and distinctly. Make simple statements and ask simple questions. Do not get overly excited and try to find out everything at once. Be tolerant of the victim's answers, which might also be repetitive or nonsensical. Be patient. Ask questions again if you are unsure of the answer. The information obtained at this time will be particularly valuable if the patient becomes less coherent or

ART RESOURCE

Although it is impossible to predict whether a person who is thinking about suicide will actually make an attempt, someone who makes it clear that he or she is contemplating this act is in obvious trouble.

unconscious later on. Ask what was taken, and how much and where the rest of the drug is. Ask if just one drug was taken. If you do not already know, try to find out where the victim's relatives and closest friends may be located. It may be important to contact them to get further information, and they may be able to provide support or make vital decisions.

Fourth, make the person feel safe. Assure him or her that you will stand by until help comes. Put the victim at ease as much as possible. This initial period is usually not a good time to ask for motives, and is never the time to make accusations.

Cardiopulmonary Resuscitation

If you find an unconscious person, after calling for help immediately check the pulse and breathing. If there is no pulse and the victim is not breathing, ideally you would begin cardiopulmonary resuscitation (CPR).

CPR is taught by schools, fire departments, and hospitals in many towns and cities across the United States. The techniques are invaluable not only for drug overdose victims but for many other medical emergencies such as near drownings and heart attacks.

If there is a pulse and the person is breathing, make sure that the airway — the path from the nose and mouth to the lungs — is clear of obstacles. This can be done by straightening the head so that there is no kink in this passageway. If the breathing sounds obstructed, look inside the mouth and check if there are any substances or secretions that can be removed.

When the victim is taken to a hospital or to a doctor's office, go with him; failing that, make sure that all the information that a doctor might need accompanies the patient. This should include everything you might know about the drug that was taken, any medical or psychiatric information you might have about the patient, and any details about other medication that the patient might have been taking. Friends and family members with knowledge of the victim should also be made available to the physician treating the victim.

After someone has tried to commit suicide and has been treated for his or her injury, a decision will be made on whether or not hospitalization is necessary. In general a hospital can provide the trained staff and suitable setting for intensive crisis intervention work, work that can focus directly both on the overdoser and the problems afflicting him or her.

A first-time suicide attempt in adolescence should never be taken lightly, even when the injury or harm done seems slight. Phrases like "It's only a gesture" or "She is only being manipulative" have no place in the evaluation of an overdoser.

For example, a teenager — call her Mary — was taken to an emergency room after overdosing with 15 aspirin. After a physical examination, she was released with the statement that her attempt was only "a superficial manipulative gesture." A week later, she was in an intensive care unit, having taken a nearly lethal overdose. No one had seen the desperation behind her first attempt. Observers had mistakenly equated the lack of medical seriousness with the lack of psychological seriousness.

Inescapable, Interminable, Intolerable

A suicidal, drug-abusing teenager looks at his or her problems

A cemetery in Newburyport, Massachusetts. The tragedy of suicide is that it wastes a life over problems that are almost always solvable.

and thinks about them in terms of what might be called the three "I's": Inescapable, Interminable, and Intolerable.

For some teenagers it is certainly understandable that they would consider their problems inescapable. These adolescents feel trapped, especially when their difficulties are centered at home. They depend on their families for food, shelter, and emotional support. Staying at home is hard, but leaving seems impossible. Drugs as an "escape" do not work, but giving them up often seems to be even worse. There appears to be no way out.

Finally, the problems seem intolerable. A suicidal teenager will often state, "I can't stand it." He or she is referring to overwhelming negative feelings.

In seeking to help someone who feels trapped in this way, there are several strategies that can be followed.

First, it is important to be aware that feeling suicidal is a valid, understandable response to emotional pain. It is also important to let the sufferer know that their pain is understood and shared. Often, suicidal people assume that their feelings are wrong but their thinking is correct. Actually, the reverse is usually the case. Their bad feelings are completely understandable in light of the troubles they are having but the solutions are wrong.

In this situation, it is advisable to let the afflicted person know that it is all right to talk openly and honestly about suicide. He or she should be encouraged to talk about it too. It is wise to ask about suicidal ideas or behavior, but suicidal behavior should always be discussed as problem-solving behavior, never as something that is sinful, vengeful, or cowardly. It is good to remember that you are there to help, not to be confrontational. Making suicidal behavior the focus of an argument or a power struggle often backfires. This can cause the affected person to feel that he or she is simply not understood.

Second, assume that behind each obvious problem stands a less obvious one that is being solved.

Paula: A Case Study

For example, Paula would frequently come home to find her parents drinking and fighting. At first they would argue, but later they would often come to blows. When this happened, Paula would run from the house and take refuge with some older, teenage friends. She would be furious with her parents and quite emotionally upset. Her friends would let her drink and would offer her drugs. Paula would get intoxicated and quite depressed. On three occasions she slit her wrists in a suicide attempt.

On the surface, it seemed that Paula's problem was the lack of an adequate way to deal with her quarreling parents. Actually, it was more complex.

Paula's parents would suddenly notice that she had run off again. They would grow angry and would call the police to find and bring back the "runaway." Her drug abuse and suicidal tendencies made it imperative that she be found. The police would locate her and bring her home or take her to an emergency room for treatment. Then, with their 14-year-old daughter safely home, the parents would stop fighting. They would also stop threatening each other and talking of

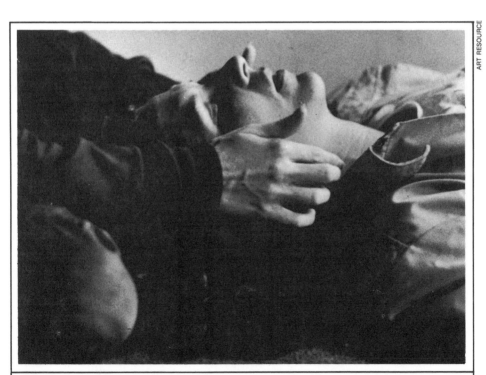

ART RESOURCE

In the aftermath of a drug overdose, support is crucial. The first thing to do after finding someone who has taken an overdose is to call for help. Next, attempt to reassure the victim that he or she is safe.

divorce. They remained angry, but no longer at each other. Now they were angry at Paula. Her behavior, however painful and destructive, was in a way "saving" the marriage. When Paula's actions were presented to the family as those of a very loyal child striving to keep the home together, the mother and father were at first shocked by the idea but eventually came to see the logic in it. For her part, Paula thought she had no other choice but to use drugs to control her emotions and to try to commit suicide as a way of coping with her troubles. As she began to understand the complexity of her family's problems, however, she began to seek viable and appropriate solutions to them. Those problems no longer seemed so Inescapable, Interminable, and Intolerable.

For Paula, her running away, drug abuse, and suicide attempts may have momentarily prevented the family from breaking up, but her actions did nothing to stop the general pattern of family friction. Needless to say, suicidal behavior is in no way a healthy or rational means of coping with conflict and difficulty. Moreover, suicide is an all too permanent

ART RESOURCE

The three "I's." Suicidal teenagers may think of their problems as Inescapable, Interminable, and Intolerable. Offering friendship and concern to those people may give them a sense that life is not really as bleak and threatening as they fear it is.

"solution" to what are most often temporary, though desperate, problems.

It is often useful to sit down and talk to a suicidal person about the problems he or she is facing. Be concrete. Ask for examples of the troubles the person is experiencing. This requires persistence and patience. The suicidal, drug-abusing teenager may not be able to talk things through at first and may speak only in generalities, such as "I feel terrible" or "Everything is awful." He or she may not believe that the conversation will do any good. "Talking things over just does not help" is an attitude often encountered at these times.

Be Ready to Listen

Providing a sounding board is often crucial. If someone is sympathetic and develops a good understanding of the emotional pain the person is trying to cope with, and if the listener is patient and persistent, the problems can usually be uncovered.

Solving the problems, however, can be hard work. It is almost never accomplished merely by willpower. At this time it is wise to avoid such advice as: "All you need to do is to stop letting things bother you so much." Instead, it is better to propose alternative solutions for each problem. It is also important to defer judgment. As the discussion proceeds, it is good to avoid trying to decide too soon which of the suggested solutions will work best. But, after a list of possible solutions has been arrived at, an approach that seems reasonable should be selected and the suicidal person should be encouraged to try it.

If the person resists and seems hopelessly stuck, he or she should be encouraged to seek professional help. School counselors, physicians, psychologists and social workers are among those who can either help directly or steer the suicidal person in the right direction.

For most people, mental states are just that, states of mind that differ from day to day and week to week. Suicidal people, however, tend to see their current problems and gloomy feelings as a permanent trait of mind, not a state of mind. "Things are the way they are, and I am the way I am" is the way they sometimes express it. Their pessimism can be frustrating. A friend may want to argue with them, to try to talk them into seeing that life can be more agreeable. This temptation to argue should be avoided. It will often lead to frustration — sometimes even to the point where the helper begins to share some of the depressed person's views. Understanding and dealing with this hopelessness may be crucial in providing help. For that reason it is vital to maintain a helpful and optimistic outlook, and to emphasize that while change may not be easy, it is possible.

Another important thing to keep in mind about seemingly intolerable feelings is that usually they are not intolerable at all. Most people can stand negative feelings and many people have developed their own tricks for dealing with difficult emotions. Taking a deep breath and counting to ten is a simple solution that has worked for many people.

In Paula's case she found that counting the cones on a large pine tree opposite her home took enough edge off her negative state of mind to enable her to look at her problems rationally. Another troubled 16-year-old developed the technique of taking a 10-minute walk and concentrating on seeing and listening to the birds.

ART RESOURCE

Helping someone who is potentially suicidal involves conveying and maintaining an optimistic attitude, emphasizing that things can improve.

Getting Psychiatric Help

Sometimes, despite such attempts at diversion, stressful, negative emotional states persist and seem to intensify. At last, they become overwhelming. In such situations, a psychiatric evaluation must be made and treatment started.

In summary, then, someone seeking to help a suicidal person should be direct in talking about suicidal behavior. It does not hurt to ask questions. Ask about drug and alcohol use. Ask about emotional symptoms, especially about depression and anxiety. If either of these conditions persists or worsens, a psychiatric evaluation is called for. Keep in touch, either by frequent personal visits or by phone calls.

Sometimes it is helpful to give someone who is potentially suicidal a card listing five or six steps to take should he or she get upset. Such a card might read:

1. Do not drink alcohol, or if drinking, STOP.
2. Walk outside, close your eyes, and take ten deep breaths.
3. Call Fred, Janet, or Neil and talk for five minutes.
4. If you do not feel better, go over to Fred's house and stay for a while.
5. Make notes about exactly what has been so upsetting.

"Talk won't help." This phrase, often heard from suicidal patients, is entirely mistaken — psychotherapy is an effective method of dealing with depression, trouble at home, and other painful problems.

ART RESOURCE

Numbers 3 and 4 on this card require some planning. A suicidal person needs friends to provide support in overcoming problems and getting through emotional bad times.

Remember, however, that you cannot totally care for a suicidal, drug-abusing teenager. Professionals in mental health care, even after years of training and practice, can feel frustrated and at a loss with these teenagers. What you can do is offer help, and perhaps the information and ideas in this book will make your efforts that much more effective, or possibly even stimulate you to come up with some techniques of your own.

People who are psychologically healthy have general feelings of well-being, as well as the ability to take pleasure in day-to-day experiences. With proper professional counseling, and support from family and friends, depression and even suicidal tendencies can be treated, alleviated, and cured.

APPENDIX

STATE AGENCIES FOR THE PREVENTION AND TREATMENT OF DRUG ABUSE

ALABAMA
Department of Mental Health
Division of Mental Illness and
  Substance Abuse Community
  Programs
200 Interstate Park Drive
P.O. Box 3710
Montgomery, AL 36193
(205) 271-9253

ALASKA
Department of Health and Social
  Services
Office of Alcoholism and Drug
  Abuse
Pouch H-05-F
Juneau, AK 99811
(907) 586-6201

ARIZONA
Department of Health Services
Division of Behavioral Health
  Services
Bureau of Community Services
Alcohol Abuse and Alcoholism
  Section
2500 East Van Buren
Phoenix, AZ 85008
(602) 255-1238

Department of Health Services
Division of Behavioral Health
  Services
Bureau of Community Services
Drug Abuse Section
2500 East Van Buren
Phoenix, AZ 85008
(602) 255-1240

ARKANSAS
Department of Human Services
Office on Alcohol and Drug Abuse
  Prevention
1515 West 7th Avenue
Suite 310
Little Rock, AR 72202
(501) 371-2603

CALIFORNIA
Department of Alcohol and Drug
  Abuse
111 Capitol Mall
Sacramento, CA 95814
(916) 445-1940

COLORADO
Department of Health
Alcohol and Drug Abuse Division
4210 East 11th Avenue
Denver, CO 80220
(303) 320-6137

CONNECTICUT
Alcohol and Drug Abuse
  Commission
999 Asylum Avenue
3rd Floor
Hartford, CT 06105
(203) 566-4145

DELAWARE
Division of Mental Health
Bureau of Alcoholism and Drug
  Abuse
1901 North Dupont Highway
Newcastle, DE 19720
(302) 421-6101

DISTRICT OF COLUMBIA
Department of Human Services
Office of Health Planning and
Development
601 Indiana Avenue, NW
Suite 500
Washington, D.C. 20004
(202) 724-5641

FLORIDA
Department of Health and
Rehabilitative Services
Alcoholic Rehabilitation Program
1317 Winewood Boulevard
Room 187A
Tallahassee, FL 32301
(904) 488-0396

Department of Health and
Rehabilitative Services
Drug Abuse Program
1317 Winewood Boulevard
Building 6, Room 155
Tallahassee, FL 32301
(904) 488-0900

GEORGIA
Department of Human Resources
Division of Mental Health and
Mental Retardation
Alcohol and Drug Section
618 Ponce De Leon Avenue, NE
Atlanta, GA 30365-2101
(404) 894-4785

HAWAII
Department of Health
Mental Health Division
Alcohol and Drug Abuse Branch
1250 Punch Bowl Street
P.O. Box 3378
Honolulu, HI 96801
(808) 548-4280

IDAHO
Department of Health and Welfare
Bureau of Preventive Medicine
Substance Abuse Section
450 West State
Boise, ID 83720
(208) 334-4368

ILLINOIS
Department of Mental Health and
Developmental Disabilities
Division of Alcoholism
160 North La Salle Street
Room 1500
Chicago, IL 60601
(312) 793-2907

Illinois Dangerous Drugs
Commission
300 North State Street
Suite 1500
Chicago, IL 60610
(312) 822-9860

INDIANA
Department of Mental Health
Division of Addiction Services
429 North Pennsylvania Street
Indianapolis, IN 46204
(317) 232-7816

IOWA
Department of Substance Abuse
505 5th Avenue
Insurance Exchange Building
Suite 202
Des Moines, IA 50319
(515) 281-3641

KANSAS
Department of Social Rehabilitation
Alcohol and Drug Abuse Services
2700 West 6th Street
Biddle Building
Topeka, KS 66606
(913) 296-3925

KENTUCKY
Cabinet for Human Resources
Department of Health Services
Substance Abuse Branch
275 East Main Street
Frankfort, KY 40601
(502) 564-2880

LOUISIANA
Department of Health and Human
  Resources
Office of Mental Health and
  Substance Abuse
655 North 5th Street
P.O. Box 4049
Baton Rouge, LA 70821
(504) 342-2565

MAINE
Department of Human Services
Office of Alcoholism and Drug
  Abuse Prevention
Bureau of Rehabilitation
32 Winthrop Street
Augusta, ME 04330
(207) 289-2781

MARYLAND
Alcoholism Control Administration
201 West Preston Street
Fourth Floor
Baltimore, MD 21201
(301) 383-2977

State Health Department
Drug Abuse Administration
201 West Preston Street
Baltimore, MD 21201
(301) 383-3312

MASSACHUSETTS
Department of Public Health
Division of Alcoholism
755 Boylston Street
Sixth Floor
Boston, MA 02116
(617) 727-1960

Department of Public Health
Division of Drug Rehabilitation
600 Washington Street
Boston, MA 02114
(617) 727-8617

MICHIGAN
Department of Public Health
Office of Substance Abuse Services
3500 North Logan Street
P.O. Box 30035
Lansing, MI 48909
(517) 373-8603

MINNESOTA
Department of Public Welfare
Chemical Dependency Program
  Division
Centennial Building
658 Cedar Street
4th Floor
Saint Paul, MN 55155
(612) 296-4614

MISSISSIPPI
Department of Mental Health
Division of Alcohol and Drug Abuse
1102 Robert E. Lee Building
Jackson, MS 39201
(601) 359-1297

MISSOURI
Department of Mental Health
Division of Alcoholism and Drug
  Abuse
2002 Missouri Boulevard
P.O. Box 687
Jefferson City, MO 65102
(314) 751-4942

MONTANA
Department of Institutions
Alcohol and Drug Abuse Division
1539 11th Avenue
Helena, MT 59620
(406) 449-2827

NEBRASKA
Department of Public Institutions
Division of Alcoholism and Drug Abuse
801 West Van Dorn Street
P.O. Box 94728
Lincoln, NB 68509
(402) 471-2851, Ext. 415

NEVADA
Department of Human Resources
Bureau of Alcohol and Drug Abuse
505 East King Street
Carson City, NV 89710
(702) 885-4790

NEW HAMPSHIRE
Department of Health and Welfare
Office of Alcohol and Drug Abuse
    Prevention
Hazen Drive
Health and Welfare Building
Concord, NH 03301
(603) 271-4627

NEW JERSEY
Department of Health
Division of Alcoholism
129 East Hanover Street CN 362
Trenton, NJ 08625
(609) 292-8949

Department of Health
Division of Narcotic and Drug Abuse
    Control
129 East Hanover Street CN 362
Trenton, NJ 08625
(609) 292-8949

NEW MEXICO
Health and Environment Department
Behavioral Services Division
Substance Abuse Bureau
725 Saint Michaels Drive
P.O. Box 968
Santa Fe, NM 87503
(505) 984-0020, Ext. 304

NEW YORK
Division of Alcoholism and Alcohol
    Abuse
194 Washington Avenue
Albany, NY 12210
(518) 474-5417

Division of Substance Abuse
    Services
Executive Park South
Box 8200
Albany, NY 12203
(518) 457-7629

NORTH CAROLINA
Department of Human Resources
Division of Mental Health, Mental
    Retardation and Substance Abuse
    Services
Alcohol and Drug Abuse Services
325 North Salisbury Street
Albemarle Building
Raleigh, NC 27611
(919) 733-4670

NORTH DAKOTA
Department of Human Services
Division of Alcoholism and Drug
    Abuse
State Capitol Building
Bismarck, ND 58505
(701) 224-2767

OHIO
Department of Health
Division of Alcoholism
246 North High Street
P.O. Box 118
Columbus, OH 43216
(614) 466-3543

Department of Mental Health
Bureau of Drug Abuse
65 South Front Street
Columbus, OH 43215
(614) 466-9023

OKLAHOMA
Department of Mental Health
Alcohol and Drug Programs
4545 North Lincoln Boulevard
Suite 100 East Terrace
P.O. Box 53277
Oklahoma City, OK 73152
(405) 521-0044

OREGON
Department of Human Resources
Mental Health Division
Office of Programs for Alcohol and
  Drug Problems
2575 Bittern Street, NE
Salem, OR 97310
(503) 378-2163

PENNSYLVANIA
Department of Health
Office of Drug and Alcohol
  Programs
Commonwealth and Forster Avenues
Health and Welfare Building
P.O. Box 90
Harrisburg, PA 17108
(717) 787-9857

RHODE ISLAND
Department of Mental Health,
  Mental Retardation and Hospitals
Division of Substance Abuse
Substance Abuse Administration
  Building
Cranston, RI 02920
(401) 464-2091

SOUTH CAROLINA
Commission on Alcohol and Drug
  Abuse
3700 Forest Drive
Columbia, SC 29204
(803) 758-2521

SOUTH DAKOTA
Department of Health
Division of Alcohol and Drug Abuse
523 East Capitol, Joe Foss Building
Pierre, SD 57501
(605) 773-4806

TENNESSEE
Department of Mental Health and
  Mental Retardation
Alcohol and Drug Abuse Services
505 Deaderick Street
James K. Polk Building, Fourth Floor
Nashville, TN 37219
(615) 741-1921

TEXAS
Commission on Alcoholism
809 Sam Houston State Office Building
Austin, TX 78701
(512) 475-2577

Department of Community Affairs
Drug Abuse Prevention Division
2015 South Interstate Highway 35
P.O. Box 13166
Austin, TX 78711
(512) 443-4100

UTAH
Department of Social Services
Division of Alcoholism and Drugs
150 West North Temple
Suite 350
P.O. Box 2500
Salt Lake City, UT 84110
(801) 533-6532

VERMONT
Agency of Human Services
Department of Social and
  Rehabilitation Services
Alcohol and Drug Abuse Division
103 South Main Street
Waterbury, VT 05676
(802) 241-2170

VIRGINIA
Department of Mental Health and
  Mental Retardation
Division of Substance Abuse
109 Governor Street
P.O. Box 1797
Richmond, VA 23214
(804) 786-5313

WASHINGTON
Department of Social and Health
  Service
Bureau of Alcohol and Substance
  Abuse
Office Building—44 W
Olympia, WA 98504
(206) 753-5866

WEST VIRGINIA
Department of Health
Office of Behavioral Health Services
Division on Alcoholism and Drug
  Abuse
1800 Washington Street East
Building 3 Room 451
Charleston, WV 25305
(304) 348-2276

WISCONSIN
Department of Health and Social
  Services
Division of Community Services
Bureau of Community Programs
Alcohol and Other Drug Abuse
  Program Office
1 West Wilson Street
P.O. Box 7851
Madison, WI 53707
(608) 266-2717

WYOMING
Alcohol and Drug Abuse Programs
Hathaway Building
Cheyenne, WY 82002
(307) 777-7115, Ext. 7118

GUAM
Mental Health & Substance Abuse
  Agency
P.O. Box 20999
Guam 96921

PUERTO RICO
Department of Addiction Control
  Services
Alcohol Abuse Programs
P.O. Box B-Y Rio Piedras Station
Rio Piedras, PR 00928
(809) 763-5014

Department of Addiction Control
  Services
Drug Abuse Programs
P.O. Box B-Y Rio Piedras Station
Rio Piedras, PR 00928
(809) 764-8140

VIRGIN ISLANDS
Division of Mental Health,
  Alcoholism & Drug Dependency
  Services
P.O. Box 7329
Saint Thomas, Virgin Islands 00801
(809) 774-7265

AMERICAN SAMOA
LBJ Tropical Medical Center
Department of Mental Health Clinic
Pago Pago, American Samoa 96799

TRUST TERRITORIES
Director of Health Services
Office of the High Commissioner
Saipan, Trust Territories 96950

Further Reading

Douglas, J.D., *The Social Meanings of Suicide*. Princeton, New Jersey: Princeton University Press, 1967.

Farmer, R., and Hirsch, S., *The Suicide Syndrome*. London: Croom Helm, 1980.

Hawton, K., and Catalan, J., *Attempted Suicide: A Practical Guide to Its Nature and Management*. Oxford: Oxford University Press, 1982.

Kreitman, N., *Parasuicide*. London: Wiley Press, 1977.

Letteiri, D.J., (ed), *Drugs and Suicide: When Other Coping Strategies Fail*. Beverly Hills, California: Sage Publications, 1978.

Offer, D., Ostrov, E., and Howard, K., *The Adolescent: A Psychological Self-Portrait*.

Schneidman, E., *Deaths of Man*. New York: Quadrangle, 1973.

Sudak, H.S., Ford, A.B., and Rushforth, N.B., (eds), *Suicide in the Young*. Boston: John Wright, 1984.

Glossary

acute situational or stress reaction   a severe emotional reaction resulting from extreme environmental stress, such as death, disaster, or similar life situations

addiction   a condition caused by repeated drug use, characterized by a compulsive urge to continue using the drug, a tendency to increase the dosage, and physiological and/or psychological dependence

alcoholism   excessive dependence on or addiction to alcohol, usually to the point that the person's physical and mental health is threatened or harmed

anomie   a condition in which an individual is not given enough guidance and feels emotionally alienated from his or her world; according to the French sociologist Émile Durkheim, anomie can lead to suicide

anxiety   an emotional state caused by uncertainty, apprehension, fear, and/or dread that produces such symptoms as sweating, agitation, and increased blood pressure and heart rate

barbiturate   a drug that causes depression of the central nervous system; generally used to reduce anxiety or to induce euphoria

bulimia   an eating disorder in which individuals periodically gorge themselves with food

cocaine   the primary psychoactive ingredient in the coca plant and a behavioral stimulant

delirium   a disturbance in the state of consciousness that stems from an acute psychological reaction characterized by restlessness, confusion, disorientation, bewilderment, and elevated blood pressure. It is associated with fear, hallucinations, and illusions

depression   a sometimes overwhelming emotional state characterized by feelings of inadequacy and hopelessness and accompanied by a decrease in physical and psychological activity

drug   any substance — plant, powder, solid, fluid, or gas — that affects bodily functions when ingested, injected, sniffed, inhaled, or absorbed into the skin

drug abuse   the use of drugs for other than legitimate medical purposes; also known as substance abuse *dysphoria*   the fundamental characteristic of depression; opposite to euphoria

euphoria   a mental high characterized by a sense of well-being

family therapy   a treatment in which an entire family meets with a therapist in order to resolve conflicts. The focus is on relationships within the family, rather than the problems of individual family members

hallucination   a sensory impression that has no basis in reality

hallucinogen   a drug that produces hallucinations

intoxication   a state of altered psychological and motor functioning caused by the ingestion of a drug

marijuana   the leaves, flowers, buds, and/or branches of the hemp plant, *Cannabis sativa* or *Cannabis indica*, that contain cannabinoids, a group of intoxicating drugs

narcotic   a drug, such as morphine or heroin, that decreases brain activity and reduces pain

overdose   ingestion of a substance in excess of any prescribed or generally recognized therapeutic dosage. An overdose can be deliberate or accidental

panic attack   an anxiety disorder characterized by rapid heartbeat, sweating, shaking, feelings of helplessness, and sometimes a fear of death

paranoia   a mental condition characterized by extreme suspiciousness, fear, delusions of persecution, and in extreme cases, hallucinations

PCP   phencyclidine; a drug first used as an anesthetic but later discontinued because of its adverse side effects; today abused for its stimulant, depressant, and/or hallucinogenic effects

physical dependence   an adaptation of the body to the presence of a drug such that its absence produces withdrawal symptoms

postvention   strategies for working with the psychological problems that may arise in a family following the suicide of one of its members

psychoactive   altering mood and/or behavior

psychological dependence   a condition in which the drug user craves a drug to maintain a sense of well-being and feels discomfort when deprived of the substance

psychosis   abnormal or pathological behavior that includes the loss of touch with reality and, in some cases, hallucinations

psychotherapy   a treatment of mental or emotional disorders using psychological methods

schizophrenia   a chronic psychotic disorder whose main symptoms include hallucinations and feelings of paranoia

sedative   a drug that produces a calming, relaxing effect

suicide ideation   thoughts of suicide, which can vary in intensity from occasional and mild to consistent and severe

suicide risk   someone who is at risk to commit suicide. To date, no certain method of determining the degree of suicide risk has been developed

suicidology   the scientific study of suicidal thinking and behavior

tolerance   a decrease in susceptibility to the effects of a drug due to its continued administration, resulting in the user's need to increase the drug dosage in order to achieve the effects experienced previously

Index

adolescence
    causes of suicide during, 31–35, 51,
       53
    drug use during, 49
    emotional turmoil during, 21–22,
       30–35
    family conflicts and, 31–32, 36–37,
       39–42, 73–75
    "parentified," 40–41
    role in family, 40–41
    romantic relationships during, 32–33
    sex roles and, 30–31
    sexual maturation and, 30
    see also behavior, suicidal; families;
       suicide
alcohol
    relation to suicide, 34–35, 37, 44,
       47–50, 59, 61–63
    see also drugs; suicide
alcoholism, 36, 43–44, 48
angel dust *see* PCP
anomie, 52
    see also suicide, risk factors
anxiety disorders, 43, 63–64
barbiturates, 49–50, 67
    see also drugs
Beck Hopelessness Inventory, 24
    see also behavior, suicidal, assessing
behavior, suicidal
    age of onset, 25, 29
    assessing, 24, 55–65
    examples, 36–37
    hospitalization, 59, 71
    therapy, 37, 58–65, 72–73, 76–79
    see also adolescence; alcohol; drugs;
       suicide
bulimia
    relation to suicide, 34–35
cardiopulmonary resuscitation (CPR), 71
    see also drugs, overdose, treatment
cocaine, 36, 67
    see also drugs
collective representation, 52
Coumadin (heparin), 67
    see also drugs
CPR *see* cardiopulmonary resuscitation

depression, 23, 43, 48, 50, 52, 63
    see also suicide, risk factors
diazepam *see* Valium
drugs
    abuse, 19, 47–51
    deaths from, 47, 67
    as means of suicide, 19, 47, 58–60
    overdose, 47, 58–61, 67
       treatment, 68–72
    relation to suicide, 48–53, 75
    side effects, 47
    see also alcohol; behavior, suicidal;
       suicide
Durkheim, Emile, 52
eating disorders *see* bulimia
families
    communication, 42
    dynamics, 39–42
    role in adolescent suicide, 31–32,
       36–37, 39–45, 56, 59, 73–75
    see also adolescence
Gandhi, Mahatma, 19
heparin *see* Coumadin
imipramine, 67
    see also drugs
marijuana, 36
    see also drugs
Menninger, Karl, 48
narcotics, 47
    see also drugs
panic disorder, 52, 63–64
PCP (phencyclidine), 47, 50, 56
    see also drugs
personality disorders, 52
    see also suicide, risk factors
phencyclidine *see* PCP
"puppy love," 32–33
schizophrenia, 52
    see also suicide, risk factors
strychnine, 67
    see also drugs
suicide
    adolescent, 20–27
    age and, 25, 29
    attitudes towards, 26–27, 35, 51,
       72–73